# A MOTHER'S BIRTH

## Rhyming my way through early motherhood

BY MARIA TEMPANY

For Terrie.
With love,
Maria Tempany
xx

# Acknowledgements

Cover illustration by: Sarah El Hassani
All Poetry Copyright
© Maria Tempany (@therhymingone)
ISBN: 978-1-5272-9-116-4
Printed by: Dublin Print Co.
www.dublinprintco.ie

Book Design: Rachel Dickens @lollysnow

Illustrations by:
Page 23, 28: Lisa Fama www.handdrawnbylisa.com
Page 32, 43: Sophie Ficek @sophsscrawls
Page 47, 61: Simona Encheva @colorful_simone
Page 53: Rachel Dickens @lollysnow
Page 81: Elizabeth Murphy @mum_doodles
Page 90: Alice Atkinson @alice_atkinson_illustration

# Dedications

To Joe, Johnny and Edie:
My inspiration. My world.

These are some tales to share with you
from pregnancy and birth, right through
those trying times, the newborn haze,
and then onto the toddler days.
What a journey, all the way,
with something new to learn each day.
The ups and downs, the lows, the highs:
We get knocked down, but we will rise.
And so I share, for what it's worth,
the story of a mother's birth.

# CONTENTS

# PREGNANCY

## That time of excited and nervous anticipation

## TO OUR BEAUTIFUL BABY

To our beautiful baby, wrapped up cozy and warm,
Here are our wishes for you:
A life full of fun, full of dreams, full of love,
And here's what we hope you will do:

Laugh every day, spread your joy in this world.
Shine a bright light far and near.
See the best in all people, the goodness that reigns.
Be kind to all those you hold dear.

Respect and trust many and, please, forgive all,
For grudges are heavy to bear.
Be yourself, find your way, in this challenging world.
Be open to change, show you care.

Success may surround you and wealth may engulf you,
But don't let them change who you are.
Follow your heart, try to do the right thing,
And we have no doubt you'll go far.

Fill your days with people who bring joy to your life,
And remember to make time for YOU.
Be curious, be brave, take a step back sometimes:
Let the power of vulnerability shine through.

Hard times WILL come, of this we are sure.
They're one thing we can't keep from you.
But what we can do is prepare you for them,
With strength and resilience too.

If you hold your head high and stay true to yourself,
You'll climb over hurdles with ease.
Should you stumble sometimes, and we've no doubt you will,
We'll help you back up off your knees.

For this life can be tough, but it's beauty shines through.
There's good all around us, you'll see.
And it will only get better when you grace this world,
Our beautiful baby-to-be!

## TO MY DARLING CHILD

To my darling child, as we wait for you:
There are so many things I'd like to do.
But the world stands still at this moment in time,
So I'll tell you a little about it in rhyme.

No-one could have known what was to come,
And it's shocked us all and frightened mum.
A virus has spread throughout the land,
And it's stopped all the things we might have planned.

But that's OK, my little one,
For all those plans can be undone.
What matters now, is the safety of all,
And we will fight this challenge standing tall.

You won't remember the worry this brought.
How across the globe, a cure was sought.
How to come back together, we all had to stay apart.
How it took the lives of many, how it broke so many hearts.

But you, my darling, have nothing to fear.
You'll continue to grow. I'll keep you safe and near.
And when you grace this world, in a few short weeks,
You'll be a ray of sunshine, in times that were bleak.

We'll huddle in close and ride this wave together.
With you on my chest, there's no storm we can't weather.
As a nation we'll pull through these tough times as one,
And rebuild all those plans that became undone.

These times will have taught us so many things:
To take nothing for granted, to value all this life brings.
The importance of touch, and the joy of a hug.
But for now little angel, keep cozy and snug.

*Written while pregnant with my daughter in the first 2020 lockdown

# THAT NEWBORN HAZE

## Filled with sleep deprivation, elation and uncertainty

## DEAR MOMMA

You're all I need in the world right now,
So hold me, momma dear.
I need your touch. I need your milk.
So please, mum, keep me near.

I know it must be hard at times,
Since I can't communicate.
I only know how to cry for now,
But I'll learn. Just you wait.

When I'm fussy or I shout a bit,
I don't mean to cause you stress.
I might have a pain, a worry,
Or need comfort from your breast.

And, mum, I know you're tired.
Your tears mix with mine at night.
It's OK: you're not alone.
After darkness, comes the light.

I won't always need you so much.
I'll grow, I'll find my way.
But for now, please hold me on your chest,
Until the break of day.

## A LOVE SO STRONG

A love so strong, hard to describe.
An animal instinct, fierce and wild.
A scary love, the all-consuming kind,
With that first touch, forever entwined.

## IS SHE GOOD?

"Is she good?" 'they' inquire, and I smile inwardly.
"No, she's awful, a terror." I mean: "Come on! Really?"

For a small little babe can't be good or be bad,
Can't explain their emotions when they're happy or sad.

"Does he sleep?" 'they' ask. "But, of course," I say.
I need not tell them he knows not night from day.

For these sweet little ones have not yet acquired,
the knowledge of time that is oh so desired.

Sleep WILL come in time. Please rest assured.
And of this 'goodness' and 'badness' they all will be cured.

But for now, while they're little, don't worry what's right or wrong,
for those small baby cuddles all too quick will be gone.

And, perhaps, maybe we should ask new mums instead:
"Can I help for an hour to let you back to bed?"

## THE STRANGEST THING

It's the strangest thing to hold someone you've grown.
It starts as a world that is oh so unknown.
A world full of fear, yet soaked in pure bliss.
Not a moment nor milestone do you want to miss.

One day you're soaring, almost walking on air.
The next, tears are flowing, and you're filled with despair.
The effort it takes to get up and get out.
Each decision you make, always laced with such doubt.

We all want our babies to flourish and thrive,
And so we take a backseat, sometimes barely survive.
What we need to remember, so that we can succeed:
Our presence and comfort is all they really need.

## A LONG NIGHT

Oh, what a night: What a long, long night.
Exhausted and I look a fright.
Hourly feeds all night long.
So weary, but I must stay strong.

She finally stills and I glance at the door.
Will I surrender to sleep or start my chores?
The former wins and I close my eyes,
When just next door, the toddler cries.

Up I yet, you know the score,
I must resolve to rest no more.
Yet another sleepless night:
I pull back the curtain and let in the light.

It's an ever challenging situation:
This seemingly endless sleep deprivation.
Maybe one day on this journey as mum,
They'll wake somewhat less and to sleep I'll succumb.

## THOSE STRIKING EYES

Those striking eyes.
That button nose.
Your big bright smile
And tiny toes.

Whatever wrongs we've done,
We did something right.
To deserve your love,
Each day and night.

*hand drawn*
BY LISA

## IN MY ARMS

Tonight in my arms as we headed to bed,
Onto my chest collapsed your sleepy head.
And I squeezed you so tight,
With all of my might.
On your dreams, I pray never, will anyone tread.

# THOSE EARLY DAYS

## Adjusting to new life

## SMILE

Small hands in our palms. Tiny heads on our chests.
These times are trying but they're surely the best.
Each day a new challenge, a true testing trial.
But small they won't stay, so let's rest here awhile.

## THAT LITTLE HAND

That little hand clasped tight in mine.
What I would give to stop the time.
To always keep her close like this.
To know there's nothing I could miss.

Yet a longing deep inside of me,
Seeks a semblance of normality.
Some time that's mine, like I had before.
Is it wrong that I'm still seeking more?

The wheels keep on turning in this parenting life,
And I want so badly to be the best mom and wife.
But the pressure I feel can engulf me sometimes,
So I put pen to paper and get lost in my rhymes.

The sleepless nights and the tantrums are tough,
And perhaps our beautiful children should just be 'enough'?
But, as I sit here with your hand clasped in mine,
Feeling nostalgic sure isn't a crime.

So, as our beautiful babies thrive and excel,
The person pre-babies needs nurture as well.
It's ok to feel sad, to experience pain.
Don't forget that all rainbows are preceded by rain.

And would I change it? Not ever!
Hard though it may be.
With your hand clasped in mine,
Is where I'm meant to be.

## THE DAY YOU WERE BORN

While we were feeding earlier,
the way we've started all your days,
I found myself reflecting
on our inaugural gaze.

A year ago today,
into this world you came.
"How did you do it on your own?"
Many people did exclaim.

I'm only now reflecting
on that distinctive night.
The fear I felt without your dad,
Worried that you'd be alright.

I felt so frightened, panic soared,
with each and every surge.
At sea. Devoid of all control:
Until that overwhelming urge

to ensure your unscathed passage
grounded me somewhat.
I brought the focus to my breath
and found that quested spot.

Soon, I had you in my arms.
Together did we cry.
Yes, it was tough without your dad,
but we did it: you and I.

•Written about birthing my daughter alone in May 2020

## CUDDLE IN

Cuddle in my little one.
I want you safe and near.
For no danger can befall you
While you're resting with me here.

Cuddle in and don't let go.
Nestle in my arm.
For here I can protect you
And you won't meet any harm.

## CAN I COME TO SEE YOUR BABY?

"Can I come to see your baby?"
Words that caused my heart to sink.
For, of course I want to see you,
But I'm weary and I stink.

It's been days since I got dressed
and there's chaos everywhere.
Dirty dishes overflowing,
and there's breast milk in my hair.

I'm really in survival mode.
I can't tell the nights from days.
My life has been uprooted
in oh so many ways.

My head feels like exploding
and I'm trying to just BE.
Yes, I've gained this new addition,
but I've lost a piece of ME.

A new love has engulfed me
and transformed my every being.
A love that, all at once,
is so constricting, and so freeing.

So, please, dear ones, I ask of you
to just give me some time
to navigate this new terrain,
that's really so sublime.

And, soon, I'll have you visit.
I can't wait for you to meet.
But, right now, all I can manage,
is to feed, sleep, and repeat.

## OUT FOR A WALK

We're out for a walk
and she's fallen asleep.
No movement at all.
Not a sound, nor a peep.

How I begged for this moment.
How I wished for this time.
To recharge the batteries,
Both hers and mine.

I think: "What will I do
with this moment of peace?"
'They' say: "Sleep when she sleeps,"
but I seek some release.

Yet, now that it's calm,
what I sought and I fought for,
Is it mad that I now miss
my sweet little daughter?!

# BREASTFEEDING RHYMES

## My Happy Place

## TEA TIME

A cup of tea while it's still hot?
A rarity more days than not.
A chance to sit and rest a while?
Never fails to bring a smile.

And while I drink, she's at the breast.
Her needs and mine are both addressed.
What a privilege it is for me,
To give food and warmth, as I sip my tea.

## CO-SLEEPING

"It must be time to put her out.
She's too dependent on you, without a doubt?"

And I think to myself that 'they' haven't a clue,
Of how special the snuggles are with you.

Yes, there are times when it isn't ideal:
I get whacked, I get kicked, with a fist or a heel.

But the comfort and closeness for me and for you,
Make co-sleeping, for now, the right thing to do.

## NIGHT FEEDS

On this topical subject, I could write a book,
but if you're looking for tips, you've got further to look.

Why do some babies wake, while others sleep through?
I'm afraid that I don't have the answers for you.

These beautiful beings are all different, you see.
They're not wired the same, much like you and like me.

Some may get hungry in the depths of the night.
With others, you blink, and they're out like a light.

For me, all the night feeds, hard though they may be,
give an unwavering sense of sweet security:

Something I've clung to in these troubled times,
when there's dark all around, but I'm yours and you're mine.

So many are craving simple touch nowadays,
so I guess we are lucky in so many ways.

And that thick fog that hovers over each tired mum,
will lift someday soon and to sleep we'll succumb.

But please know, in the meantime, when you're up in the night,
you're not alone in that tunnel which will soon flood with light,

and I have a strong feeling that in times to come:
we'll miss these precious moments, just baby and mum.

## BOND

My god do I savour
Each and every feed.
You cuddle in close,
And I'm all that you need.

The bond that we share
Is second to none.
I'm so honoured and humbled
To be who you'll call mum.

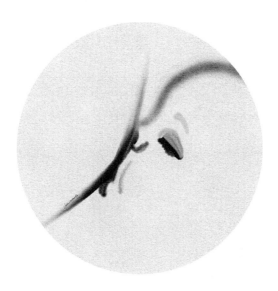

## YES, I FEED MY CHILD TO SLEEP

Yes, I feed my child to sleep,
and no, I do not care
if in the eyes of others
it means 'dependency' is there.

For, of course they are dependant,
sure we are the world to them.
And if she wakes another time,
I'll feed her yet again.

As the comfort that it gives her
is a privilege I bear,
and I'll continue to soothe her,
while her need for me is there.

## I'LL FEED HER ANYWHERE

Yes, I'll feed her anywhere.
At a restaurant? In the park?
No, location does not matter.
Be it daytime, be it dark.

For, wherever we may travel,
her food source ventures too.
To soothe her anytime of day:
Drinks on tap? A dream come true!

## OUR FOOLPROOF TECHNIQUE

I guess I'll have to stop this soon.
I can't feed to sleep next week.
But you don't know any other way.
It's been our foolproof technique.

Each time I put you down to sleep,
Be it day or be it night.
We cuddle up, and you latch on,
And you're out like a light.

They've been some of our best moments,
Our eyes locked before yours shut.
And I gaze on a little longer,
Praying you'll never be hurt.

What innocence you radiate,
And times like these don't keep.
So, I'll cross this bridge another day.
For now, let's feed to sleep.

# A Mother's birth

# A GROWING FAMILY

Evolving each day

## JUST US

We began with just two, now we're a family of four.
And it's hard to make time for 'just us' anymore.

All those weekends away, now a thing of the past.
The hotels, the spa breaks, we sure had a blast.

The leisurely lie-ins, with coffee in bed.
All now replaced, with early rises instead.

To lie on the couch and feel your hand in mine,
Will we do that again? When will we realign?

For this beautiful family we've created in love,
We're so grateful and, yes, we thank the stars above.

But there's times when I miss the 'just us' days:
When I'd blush and I'd smile under your radiant gaze.

So, I vow to make time for my soulmate once more,
And to rebuild the couple that we were before.

## WHEN THREE BECOME FOUR

It's such a change for our babies, when three become four.
They wake up one morning and they're the baby no more.

They've had us all to themselves, for the whole life they've known.
And then, all of a sudden, their family has grown.

With those new arrivals, our expectation increases:
"You're a big boy now, sweetheart, come help pick up the pieces."

We can't comprehend how much their life has changed.
Everything that they've known has now been rearranged.

And they can't yet express all the thoughts in their head,
So the tantrums now jump to the forefront instead.

While we might feel frustrated, it's our role to remind:
"You are loved more than ever. You'll never be left behind."

So, my darling, we need you more than ever before.
And we'll all grow together, as this family of four.

## STORMY SEAS

Two sleeping babies:
Not an easy feat!
Some time, just us, to rest a bit,
And, goodness, is it sweet.

'They' say the early years are tough.
Relationships are tested.
Everyone is sleep deprived,
Fed up and never rested.

While many things 'they' say are wrong,
This one sure rings true.
Life no longer bears resemblance
To the days of me and you.

While I know we push each other,
To the brink more days than not,
My love then can't hold a candle
To the love that I've now got.

From best friend and lifetime partner,
To now ever present dad.
You surprise me every day with
Traits I never knew you had.

So, as we navigate these
Stormy seas and foreign lands,
We'll emerge stronger than ever,
Together, hand in hand.

# A Mother's birth

## DADS

This one's a little different: It's for all the dads out there.
To say we love you very much, lest you thought we didn't care.

Momma bear may rule the roost, but you play a crucial part.
Watching you become a dad, has been a revelation from the start.

No-one could have told me, the father you'd become,
The support that you would offer, to help me blossom as mum.

While I may take the reins at times, your strength does lead the way.
I get bogged down in all the chores, while you get engrossed in play.

And when they see their daddy dear, their little eyes light up.
Though challenging, I think it's clear: Parenthood has filled our cup!

So, thanks for showing me the joy that fatherhood has brought you.
And with their deep devoted love, we've evolved from just us two.

## SHOUT OUT TO THE HUSBANDS

Shout out to the husbands
Who bring us tea in bed.
They can prove to all the world
That chivalry's not dead.

Now rest assured this doesn't happen
Every single day.
I'm often told – "Haha, my love,
You're not in luck today."

But on these rare occasions,
It sure feels like a win:
To enjoy a cup of tea in bed,
Before the day begins.

# MOTHERHOOD WOES

That struggle with body image,
juggling it all and
managing expectations

## HOW IS IT ONLY LUNCHTIME?

How is it only lunchtime?
What a morning we have had!
It started off quite good in fact.
How could it have turned so bad?

Off to the park we headed.
Promises of puddles galore!
A happy boy and sweet baby:
what treats had we in store.

Lots of splashes, so much fun.
"He's so cute," said passers-by.
When the little one woke with a start,
and, my goodness, did she cry!

And, just as she latched at the breast,
this moment he did choose
to sit down in the muddy grass
and take off both his shoes!

The roars then sure did follow
as he kicked and hit the ground.
A busy day up at the park,
lots of people all around.

"Come on," I pleaded.
"Time to go. Just stop being so bold."
I surprised myself by shouting that.
How could I have been so cold?

For I try to 'gentle parent'.
At least, I do give it a go.
But, I'm not perfect, that's for sure.
Hence this age old tale of woe!

Thank you to the lady
who stopped as my tears fell.
"Can I help?" she asked.
"Are you OK? I remember it all so well."

At first I felt so guilty:
she must have heard me yell.
And her kindness took me by surprise.
My eyes continued to swell.

"Thanks," I muttered through the tears,
"His nap is nearly due."
"It's so tough," she said,
"You're doing great. Oh the joy of being two!"

She smiled in solidarity
and we headed on our way.
Time to pour some tea and rest these feet:
Tomorrow is another day!

BEAUTIFUL

The top may say 'beautiful' but I feel anything but.
It would be much more apt if it said 'stuck in a rut.'
My clothes just won't fit and I can't stop the binging.
I catch a glance in the mirror and I can't keep from cringing.

Then I look at the bundle of joy in my arm.
Not a thing I won't do to keep her from harm.
And while days roll into nights on this parenting wheel,
I know that 'beautiful' is just how I want HER to feel.

And how will she learn if I put myself down?
How will self-love engulf her, if in insults I drown?
So, it's time to stop slating myself in this way.
Beauty shines from within and not by what you weigh.

So, in fact, a reminder to me and to you:
We're all beautiful mommas, we must let it shine through!
Try to show self-compassion and allow some leeway.
We've made these gorgeous babies at the end of the day.

## CONTRADICTIONS

I would hold you forever
In the nook of my arm
Wrapped up cozy and snug:
Free from pain, free from harm.

Though perhaps that's not fair,
To keep you as you are,
When the wonder of you
Could reach ever so far.

It's a strange contradiction,
These thoughts we all share.
Longing to keep them close,
Yet encourage their flair.

We instil independence,
But pray they won't venture far.
Foster courage, yet crave reliance
Wherever they are.

Oh, I know I can't keep you,
So little, like this.
With your head on my chest,
Nothing short of pure bliss.

So, I'll help grow your wings.
With pride, I'll watch you shine.
But, for now, little angel,
You are truly all mine.

## ONLY MUM

Who needs make-up or hair done?
Who needs a shower when you're 'only mum'?

It's hard to feel like you sometimes.
Days roll into nights and blur the lines.

When you're swamped in nappies and baby-gros,
Time for you? Out the window it goes!

Oodles of coffee and a cry behind closed doors,
Help a little to lessen the roars!

But it's the best job of all at the end of the day.
And those heart-warming smiles take the pain away.

## PUT THE PHONE AWAY

I got a rude awakening when my son said to me today
With a look so earnest in his eyes: "Mama, put the phone away."

I was rooted to that very spot, when, yet again, he said:
"Mama, put it down, right over there, come play with me instead."

A sense of shame engulfed me, and all at once I knew
That HE had the right idea, despite his ripe old age of two.

As instructed, down I got, to play with my sweet boy.
To dissipate that shame I felt. To replace it with pure joy.

What affirmations we may seek, behind these screens we all possess,
Can often be a source of pain, upset and much distress.

Did anybody like my post? A follow? Or a share?
Quite frankly, and perhaps he's right, my son really doesn't care.

Of course all these communities have a crucial role to play.
Especially in the times we're in, with those we love at bay.

But, for me, this simple statement from the centre of MY world,
Struck a cord so painfully, I felt compelled to share this word.

So, one and all, why don't we try to 'put the phones away'.
Not all the time, just now and then, and, ever present, try to stay.

## THE ONE IN THE MIRROR

Who is that person peering right back at me?
Standing just where my reflection should be.
That can't be me, for this girl looks so weary.
And, why, oh why, are her green eyes so teary?

She's aged and she's changed.
Her hair's been rearranged.
Her clothes look a bit tight,
And those bags are a fright.

But, despite all of that, there's a glow about her.
A fire that's igniting, with emotions to stir.
And, when I glance again, a little longer this time,
There's a gleam in those eyes that reminds me of mine.

Yes, she's been changed. Irrevocably.
But, she's still there, still present, about to break free.
"I see you." I tell her, "It took time, but I see."
I'll now open my heart to this new version of me.

## THE IMMINENT RETURN TO WORK

One week to go.
Time is sure moving on.
The leave that seemed lengthy
all too soon is now gone.

There's a thing they call work
that's dragging me back.
Please tell me I'm dreaming.
Please say it's a hack.

For I don't want to leave you,
Not you nor your brother.
And all that matters to me
is to be the best mother.

What if you need me?
And you find I'm not there?
Can your young minds grasp
That, though absent, I care

More than anything else
in this bittersweet world,
That all cries be answered
For my boy and my girl.

But I will return
And in my job I'll survive.
And I know that my darlings
Will continue to thrive.

And I'll be ever present,
With you both from afar,
For my heart will remain
Where my babies are.

The most important job
that I'll ever do,
Is become my best version
of mum to you.

# THOSE
# TRYING TIMES

## The endless chores

## THE LAUNDRY MOUNTS

The laundry mounts and the plates pile high.
Time seems to stand still and yet the days fly by.
How do such little people create so much mess?
Endless clothes to fold, dirty floors to address.

"It's the chaos of new parenthood," 'they' say.
"It'll all go so fast. Don't wish it away."
So, I try and I try to soak it all in,
To cherish each moment, to summon patience within.

But there's no denying how hard it can be,
To turn away from the chaos, and to really SEE,
The things they keep throwing shows the strength they've acquired.
The paints on the floor, show how they feel inspired!

It's a barrel of laughs and a crate full of tears.
Each day full of hope, full of dreams, full of fears.
This parenting role, is the toughest to face,
But, my goodness, there's nothing like your child's embrace.

## WILL THERE ALWAYS BE?

Will there always be endless clothes to fold?
Toys to put away? A dishwasher to load?

I feel like the chores are just on repeat.
Targets to reach and goals I can't meet.

And I know that I probably need to slow down,
To sit with the mess, or in the chaos I'll drown.

A skill I require is to be still and rest,
To take it all in but it's such a hard test.

The running and racing will soon take its toll,
I should read a good book, or perhaps take a stroll.

As the kids won't remember, the super clean floors.
They won't recall if mum did all her chores.

But the play and the stories, their memories will make.
So I'll focus on that for everyone's sake!

No jobs today? I'll happily oblige,
And give them what matters in their little eyes.

## ONE OF THOSE DAYS

It's been one of those days.
I'm about to explode.
Feeling broken, exhausted,
I might crack with the load.

She won't sleep, not a bit,
And he won't stop the crying.
And I know I need patience,
But believe me, I'm trying.

What do they want?
For I can't give much more.
And it scares me to think
What they might have in store!

And I know I'm so lucky,
Heaven knows that I'm blessed.
But it's OK to struggle,
And we all can feel stressed.

Time for a bath and
Deep breaths in and out.
Time to summon the strength,
That is there, without doubt.

To remind myself how
They don't mean to upset,
And that these days are numbered:
There's no need to fret.

For after the bad days,
Come plenty of good.
Things will realign
in the way that they should!

And their smiles will endear us,
Render joy like before.
Otherwise, there's no chance,
We would have any more!

## NEGOTIATIONS

You want a shower? Well, I need a walk.
If you tackle bedtime, maybe then we can talk.

I'm tried and I'm cranky. MY needs aren't met.
I did the LAST nappy, lest you dare to forget.

Did I sign up for this? All the negotiation?
I'll trade you a shower for some appreciation.

We're both trying our best, that can't be denied.
But that doesn't give you a licence to hide

When that familiar smell wafts through the air.
You've a phone call to make? I'm afraid I don't care!

To sum it all up, it's been one of those days.
I've been pulled, I've been pushed in oh so many ways.

When I need a rant, you're the only one here.
Through the good and the bad times, you pledged to stay near.

This is one of the latter, so listen you must:
To my nagging and moaning, or I soon might combust.

And later we'll laugh when they're tucked up in bed,
As we prepare and plan for the day that's ahead.

More of the same? But it's better together.
United we'll stay and these days we shall weather.

## LET MOTHER'S LOVE PREVAIL

We all will traverse different paths,
On this road we face as 'mother'.
The things that challenge me the most
May be easy for another.

Feeding might come naturally,
Or be an awful struggle.
Some may find those sleepless nights
The toughest thing to juggle.

For others, it may be the fact
That everything has changed.
Besotted with their little ones,
But from themselves estranged.

Despite these many differences,
There is one certain thing:
Nothing could prepare us for
The love these babies bring.

So, look within and trust YOUR heart,
Let instinct guide you through.
For only YOU know what is best
For your baby and you.

Turn off all the noise of those
Who think they know YOUR trail.
You'll find the route that's right for you,
Let mother's love prevail.

# TODDLER LIFE

## The not-so-terrible twos

## IN THE BLINK OF AN EYE

And, just like that, in the blink of an eye,
Our baby turns two and shouts "mama, bye bye."

And I think of the nights in the early days,
When you'd cling onto me and we'd ride sleepless waves.

I couldn't see then, the brave boy you'd become.
The joy that you'd bring us: the laughs, all the fun.

The love that you've sown in our hearts that keeps growing,
The marks on the walls from the toys you keep throwing!

So, while my heart breaks a little, each time you push me away,
I know you're just learning, just finding your way.

And I'll take the side-lines to watch you shine in the light,
But know that I'm here, every day, every night.

So, continue to flourish my sweet little boy.
Thanks for making me mum. You're my pride and my joy.

## BIG AND STRONG

Tonight your bright eyes shone for me,
like you could do no wrong.
And you told me with a sense of pride:
"Mama, I'm now big and strong."

I said "Yes, my dear, you surely are,
and you make me proud each day."
May that confidence that you exude,
Guide you on your way.

And may all the hurdles that life throws,
just help you learn and grow.
So, sleep soundly love, and rest assured:
You're the strongest boy I know.

## VULNERABILITY

While we were walking earlier,
our daily outing to the park,
the playground, followed by the pond,
"I see the ducks," you do remark.

A thought just struck me like a blow,
as you ran so wild and free:
If only I could bottle up
your vulnerability.

Brave, yet so dependent,
Constant knowledge do you seek,
For vulnerability has such strength,
although some may think it weak.

You bare unfiltered and so raw
your toddler emotions.
That transparency and openness
would make some powerful potions.

For, all too often, we do hide
behind a mask of pure pretence.
When, to speak our truth with honesty,
would make so much more sense.

A Mother's birth

So, perhaps, our little toddlers
can teach both me and you,
to remove that mask and to allow
the power of vulnerability shine through.

## MAMA, YOU CALL

"Mama," you call,
in the depths of the night.
Sometimes soft, sometimes sharp,
sometimes pained with your plight.

A dreadful dream or a fear,
that stirred you from sleep?
"Don't worry my darling,"
From my bed I do leap.

I'm tired and weary but
your needs are my own.
I won't rest a minute
whilst you're crying alone.

With one touch I soothe you,
Cradle you in my arm.
It's my role to protect you,
keep you free from harm.

"Just leave her a minute.
She'll settle in time."
The musings of some,
but those views are not mine.

Why leave her afraid
when my touch has the cure?
All she seeks is my comfort.
Why should stress she endure?

So, though tired and weary,
I'll continue to come,
to your side with each call,
for your safe place is mum.

## YOU MAY ONLY BE TWO

You may only be two
but, my goodness, you've grown.
Yes, you'd have us believe,
you can do it alone!

"Go away momma.
No I won't hold your hand."
And in all disagreements,
Your ground you will stand!

And then evening time falls:
"It's getting dark now," you say.
Bravery and independence
Shrink right away.

Time for a book.
"Momma, read me a story."
Still wet from the bath
Standing in all your glory.

And you snuggle in close,
let me squeeze you so tight.
My favourite time of the day,
Before we say good night.

So you may now be two,
But you're still little to me.
And I'll treasure each moment,
On this special journey.

## LET'S BUILD A CASTLE

I've got the kids on my own
and my mum's not around,
And to add to the stress
Rain is pounding the ground.

Will I even get dressed?
What's the point? So much hassle?
Then those bright eyes light up
and say: "Let's build a castle."

Getting down on the ground,
To your level, your world,
Snaps me out of the fog,
Into beauty unfurled.

Your imagination blossoms,
And I get drawn right in,
Telling stories of splendour
With a creative spin.

And with your little finger
Pointing out all the wonder,
We'll weather all storms,
Even lightning and thunder.

YOUR SAFE SPACE

When your little mind is weary and
Your bright eyes are all teary.
I hope you'll always find in me a space,
To feel at ease in my embrace.

## BABIES NO MORE

With each passing day,
To new heights you soar.
And sometimes it seems
That you're babies no more.

But, forever, dear angels,
My babies you'll be.
May your wings fly you high
And then home here to me.

# SELF-CARE

A gentle reminder

its ok to believe in yourself

## KIND

Be kind and show compassion
In everything you do.
But, don't forget, above all else,
That kindness starts with you.

## IN THE DARKNESS OF THE NIGHT

In the darkness of the night,
There's a stillness everywhere.
A time to pause, reflect and muse,
On that thing they call self-care.

Did I do enough for me today?
Did I stop and take the time
To fill MY cup, or, once again,
Did YOUR needs triumph mine?

I'm sure we can all raise a hand
And admit to so much hurry.
Completing tasks with urgency,
Feeling overwhelmed with worry.

What we need to do is pause sometimes
And take a little rest.
To reflect on the resounding fact
That we can only do our best.

If we've got other souls to nourish,
Cherished ones to help and mind.
We're no good unless we mind ourselves,
So, please, to yourself, be kind.

# FIGHTER

Free yourself from obligations.
Pull your boundaries a little tighter.
Let all those worries float away.
Soon you will feel lighter.

## A SLUMBER SO DEEP

It's late and I guess I should soon go to sleep.
My body is craving a slumber so deep.
My mind is tired. I have heavy eyes.
To surrender to sleep would surely be wise.

But in this moment of stillness, I do want to stay.
Unsummoned. Unpressured. At peace, you might say.
So while that urge to sleep surges stronger and stronger,
I'll sit here and linger a little bit longer.

# A Mother's birth

# About the Author

Maria is a medical doctor and mum of two from Dublin, Ireland.

Rhyming poetry has always been a passion of hers,
and the arrival of her children in recent years
has spurred on that creative streak.

'A Mother's Birth' is her first book about the ever
tumultuous journey that is early motherhood.

More of her poetry can be found under
the alias of @therhymingone on social media.